Mammals

The Nature Company Discoveries Library published by Time-Life Books

Conceived and produced by
Weldon Owen Pty Limited
43 Victoria Street, McMahons Point,
NSW, 2060, Australia
A member of the
Weldon Owen Group of Companies
Sydney • San Francisco
Copyright © 1996 US Weldon Owen Inc.
Copyright © 1996 Weldon Owen Pty Limited
Reprinted 1997

THE NATURE COMPANY
Priscilla Wrubel, Ed Strobin, Steve Manning,
Georganne Papac, Tracy Fortini

TIME-LIFE BOOKS
Time-Life Books is a division of Time Life Inc.
Time-Life is a trademark of Time Warner Inc.
U.S.A.

Time-Life Custom Publishing
Vice President and Publisher: Terry Newell
Director of New Product Development:
Quentin McAndrew
Managing Editor: Donia Ann Steele
Director of Sales: Neil Levin
Director of Financial Operations: J. Brian Birky

WELDON OWEN Pty Limited
Chairman: Kevin Weldon
President: John Owen
Publisher: Sheena Coupe
Managing Editor: Rosemary McDonald
Project Editor: Helen Bateman
Text Editor: Claire Craig
Art Director: Sue Burk
Designer: Nicole Court
Assistant Designer: Melissa Wilton
Visual Research Coordinator: Jenny Mills
Photo Research: Annette Crueger

Illustrations Research: Peter Barker
Production Manager: Caroline Webber
Production Assistant: Kylie Lawson
Vice President, International Sales:
Stuart Laurence
Coeditions Director: Derek Barton

Text: Carson Creagh

Illustrators: Alistair Barnard; André Boos;
Martin Camm; Simone End; Christer Eriksson;
Tim Hayward/Bernard Thornton Artists, UK;
David Kirshner; Frank Knight; John Mac/Folio;
James McKinnon; Trevor Ruth; Peter Schouten;
Kevin Stead; Rod Westblade

Library of Congress
Cataloging-in-Publication Data
Creagh, Carson.
Mammals / Carson Creagh.

     p. cm.-- (Discoveries Library)

  Includes index.
  ISBN 0-8094-9372-1
  1. Mammals--Juvenile literature.
  [1. Mammals.] I. Title. II. Series.
QL706.2.C74 1996
599--dc20   95-32820

Manufactured by Mandarin Offset
Printed in China

A Weldon Owen Production

Mammals

CONSULTING EDITOR

Dr. George McKay

Senior Lecturer, School of Biological Sciences
Macquarie University, Sydney, Australia

Contents

FAMILY LIFE
Lions are typical mammals in many ways. Their bodies have fur, they work together to find food, and their young need to be cared for and fed with milk. Mammals look after their young longer than other vertebrates do. Lion cubs continue to nurse for up to six months.

SLEEPING OVER
Because food is scarce in winter, many mammals conserve energy and live off the fat stored in their bodies by sleeping for long periods. This is called hibernation. It lowers their body temperature, heartbeat and breathing.

• THE WORLD OF MAMMALS •

Introducing Mammals

Most of the animals we keep as pets, such as dogs, cats and rabbits, and the animals we use for work, such as horses, are mammals. Humans are mammals too. Mammals belong to a group of animals called vertebrates, all of which have backbones. They are warm-blooded, which means they have a constant body temperature, no matter how cold or hot their surroundings may be. There are nearly 4,000 species of mammal, and most of these have hair or fur on their bodies. Except for the platypus and echidna, all mammals give birth to live young. Unlike other animals, they feed their young with milk. Mammals evolved from reptiles that had several bones in the lower jaw, but mammals have only one bone in the lower jaw.

EARS AND NOSES
The African aardvark has a large nose and big ears. Like many other mammals, it has a well-developed sense of smell and good hearing.

GROWL!
Like many other mammals, wolves work together to find food. This wolf is baring its sharp teeth to let other wolves know that it is angry.

TYPES OF MAMMAL

The three main groups of mammal are monotremes, marsupials and placental mammals. Monotremes (the platypus and echidna) have many features in common with mammals' reptile ancestors. They have a single opening, called a cloaca, for reproduction and body wastes, and they lay eggs. Female marsupials, such as opossums and wallabies, give birth to young that are not fully developed, and are protected in pouches until they can fend for themselves. The young of placental mammals, such as bushbabies, are fed inside the females' bodies by a special organ called a placenta and are more developed than marsupials when born.

Platypus

Rock wallaby

Bushbaby

DID YOU KNOW?

The smaller the mammal, the faster the heartbeat. In one minute, a shrew's heart beats about 200 times, a human's heart beats about 65 times and an elephant's heart beats about 25 times.

7

BREAK-OUT
The odd-looking star-nosed mole from North America uses its spadelike front feet to dig through the soil. It detects its prey of worms and insects with its sensitive star-shaped nose.

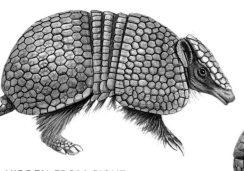

HIDDEN FROM SIGHT
The three-banded armadillo searches for food at night. But if it is attacked by a predator, such as a puma, it rolls into a ball and uses its horny skin as armor plating.

Designs for Living

Mammals are among the most successful animals ever to have lived. Because they are warm-blooded, they can survive in almost any environment. To take advantage of different environments, mammals have evolved different body shapes. They have adapted to life in the jungles, deserts and high mountains; in the polar regions; in the air and in the trees; beneath the ground and in the oceans. They have also adapted as they moved from one environment to another. The ancestors of today's horses, for example, lived in forests and were small enough to move among trees and undergrowth. When they began to live on the open plains, however, they grew larger and stronger so they could migrate in search of fresh food, and faster so they could escape the fast-moving predators of the plains.

Gray-headed fruit bat (male/female)
Length: 11 in (28 cm)
Wingspan: 2 ft 7 in (80 cm)
Weight: 2 lb (800 g)

Gorilla (male)
Height: (standing on knuckles) 5 ft 3 in (1.62 m)
Weight: 375 lb (170 kg)

Human (female)
Height: 5 ft 2 in (1.59 m)
Weight: 110 lb (50 kg)

Black-handed spider monkey (female)
Height: up to 2 ft (60 cm)
Weight: 9 lb (4 kg)

ALL SHAPES AND SIZES
Mammals have evolved different body shapes to allow them to live in almost every kind of environment. The sizes given here are the averages for each of these mammals.

Blue whale (female)
Length: 91 ft (28 m)
Weight: 91 tons (90 tonnes)

Australian sea lion (male)
Length: 6 ft 8 in (2.1 m)
Weight: 660 lb (300 kg)

Gemsbok (male)
Height: 4 ft (1.2 m)
Weight: 450 lb (204 kg)

LOOKING ALIKE

Some mammals look similar and live in similar ways even though they are not related to each other and live in different parts of the world. Scientists call this convergent evolution. Many Australian mammals have evolved to resemble unrelated mammals in other parts of the world. The striped possum has a long, narrow finger just like that of the aye-aye from Madagascar. They both hook grubs out of holes in trees with their long fingers. Like the pangolins of Africa and Asia, echidnas have long noses, long sticky tongues and no teeth. Koalas look similar to the sloths of Central and South America. Both live in trees, eat leaves and move slowly.

Aye-aye

Striped possum

Short-beaked echidna

Pangolin

Koala

Sloth

TREE GLIDING
Despite their name, flying squirrels cannot fly. They glide from tree to tree, tightening a flap of skin between their front and back legs, which acts like a parachute.

WINTER COAT
Mammals that live in harsh environments, such as the Arctic, adapt to different seasons by changing color. The Arctic fox has a brown coat in summer, but grows a white coat for camouflage in winter.

Giraffe (male)
Height: 16 ft (4.95 m)
Weight: 2,600 lb (1,180 kg)

African elephant (male)
Height: 11 ft (3.35 m)
Weight: 5 tons (5.1 tonnes)

Black rhinoceros (male)
Height: 5 ft (1.52 m)
Weight: 1¼ tons (1.3 tonnes)

Beaver (male/female)
Length: 3 ft 3 in (1 m)
Weight: 66 lb (30 kg)

Discover more in Finding Food

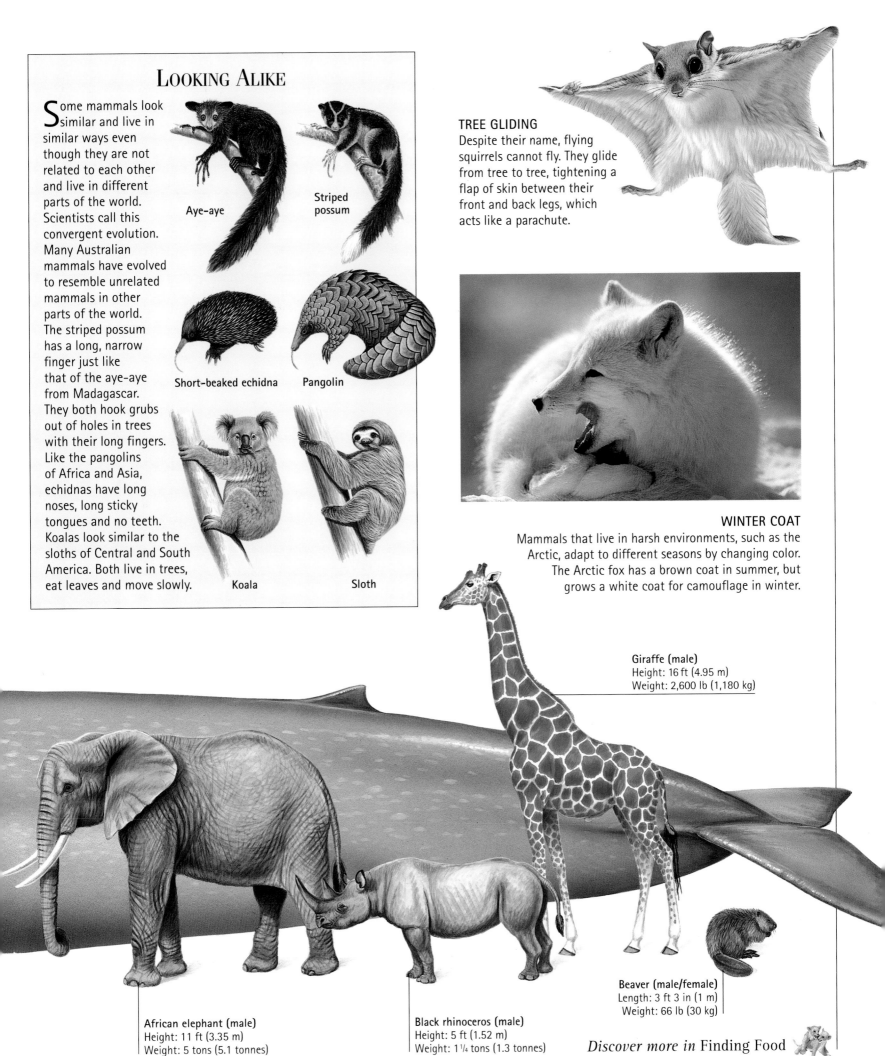

PICTURING A MAMMAL
Fossilized bones provide clues to the appearance of an extinct mammal. From them, we can reconstruct a model such as this tree-dwelling *Thylacoleo,* a meat-eating relative of today's kangaroo.

• THE WORLD OF MAMMALS •

Mammal Beginnings

The first mammals were small, shrewlike animals that were about 5 in (12 cm) long. Related to today's monotremes, they first appeared during the Triassic Period, about 220 million years ago. They were descended from reptiles called synapsids, which appeared about 300 million years ago. These primitive mammals evolved into different groups during the Jurassic and Cretaceous periods (208–65 million years ago). Most of these early mammals were carnivores (meat eaters), but some, such as the tree-living multituberculates, which ranged from animals the size of mice to some as big as beavers, ate plants. The ancestors of today's marsupials, insectivores and primates first appeared in the Cretaceous Period (145–65 million years ago). When the dinosaurs died out at the end of the Cretaceous Period, these modern mammals spread to every continent and evolved into thousands of new species.

DID YOU KNOW?
Camels and their near relatives now live in South America, Asia and Africa. They evolved in North America but died out there during the Pleistocene Period, about 12,000 years ago.

SPIKY ANCESTOR
Sail-backed *Dimetrodon* was a mammal-like reptile. It belonged to a group of animals that had large openings in their skulls behind the eye sockets. Mammals gradually evolved from members of this group.

THE FIRST MAMMAL

Megazostrodon, which lived in Africa about 220 million years ago, is the oldest known mammal. This insect eater was only 5 in (12 cm) long and probably laid eggs like today's monotremes.

FIRST PERSON

The earliest known human was *Australopithecus afarensis*, who lived in northern Africa about 3 million years ago. About 4 ft (1.2 m) tall, *Australopithecus* was first identified from a series of footprints found in hardened volcanic ash. In 1974, the skeleton of a female *Australopithecus*, named "Lucy" by its discoverers, was found in Ethiopia.

CIRCLING THEIR PREY

On the plains of northern Africa 40 million years ago, a female *Arsinoitherium* defends her young against a pack of 4-ft (1.2-m) long predators called *Hyaenodon*. Although *Arsinoitherium* grew to nearly 13 ft (4 m) long, they were actually relatives of today's rabbit-sized hyraxes.

Hyenas are scavengers during the day and wait to feed on animals killed by lions. At night, however, they become hunters themselves!

• THE WORLD OF MAMMALS •

Finding Food

Mammals use many different strategies to find food. Some mammals are hunters, while others are scavengers and dine on leftovers. Some migrate in search of food and others hoard food for winter. Mammals eat almost anything, from plants to other mammals. Vampire bats live on blood, echidnas eat ants and a pack of wolves will eat a moose or other large mammal. The amount of food a mammal eats varies greatly. Very small mammals cannot store much energy and warmth inside their bodies. Because they lose energy quickly, they have to eat a lot of food. A shrew, for example, must eat more than its own body weight every day or it will freeze to death. Strangely enough, the largest mammal—the whale—also eats large amounts of food. This is because it grows quickly (a newborn blue whale gains about 200 lb [90 kg] every day!) and because it has to swim long distances in search of food.

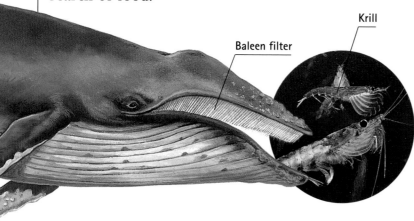

Krill

Baleen filter

FILTERING THROUGH
Baleen whales have long, fringed plates of horny baleen instead of teeth. They filter hundreds of 2-in (5-cm) long shrimp called krill through the baleen and trap them inside their mouths.

ON THE MOVE

Many plant-eating mammals migrate to where their food is plentiful. Reindeer in the Arctic travel away from the snow in search of fresh green grass.

DESERT DINING

The gerenuk, or giraffe-gazelle, lives in eastern Africa. It is so well adapted to life in the desert that it never needs to drink. With the help of its long neck, it gets enough moisture from the tender leaves of prickly bushes and trees.

SAVING UP

Squirrels collect nuts and seeds and hide them in hollow trees. They save them to eat during long winters and to have a supply of food ready for the spring.

HUNTING TOGETHER

Many carnivorous mammals cooperate to find food—even humpback whales work together to herd schools of fish. Dolphins, porpoises and seals, lions, hyenas, wolves and other dogs work together to save the energy of individual hunters and to make sure that every member of the group eats enough to survive. Here, a group of African wild dogs corners a wildebeest.

13

Mammal Society

PART OF A GROUP
Meerkats are very sociable and live together in packs. Living in a group makes it easier to defend the pack and care for the young.

S ome mammals, such as bears, orang-utans and koalas, are solitary animals. They live alone and only come together to mate. But most mammals are social and live in groups. Living in groups has many advantages. Mammals that might be preyed on by birds, reptiles or other mammals can defend each other and their young. Because a predator has many targets to choose from in a group, most members have time to escape. Humans are the only mammals who use words to communicate. Other social animals use smells, facial expressions or body language to "talk" to each other. Dogs, for example, wag their tails when they are happy, and snarl, bare their teeth and growl when they are being aggressive. Most mammals communicate to tell other members of the group how they are feeling, or to warn them of danger.

MORE FOR SHOW
Serious fights are rare among social animals. Male elephant seals push, roar and slash each other, but they seldom do real harm.

GETTING TO KNOW YOU
Social mammals spend a lot of time getting to know each other before they mate, because most species bring up the young together.

Bringing Up the Family
Gibbons live in South and Southeast Asia. They are social apes and move through the tree tops in family groups, searching for fruits, grubs, insects and leaves. The young take two years to wean, but they stay with the family until they are fully mature and help to take care of their younger siblings.

Platypuses and Echidnas

COVER UP
Strong muscles control a fold of skin that tightens to cover the platypus's eyes and ears when it dives. Instead of sight and sound, it uses its sensitive bill to find its way underwater.

The Australian platypus, the short-beaked echidna of Australia and New Guinea, and the New Guinea long-beaked echidna are monotremes. These very primitive mammals have many reptile features, such as a cloaca, which is used to get rid of body wastes and to lay eggs. These mammals ooze milk for their young from special patches of skin. Both platypuses and echidnas have a lower body temperature than other mammals, and echidnas hibernate in winter. Male platypuses and echidnas have a long spur on each hind leg. In platypuses, this is connected to a venom gland and is used in fights between males. Special organs in the rubbery skin of the platypus's bill can detect the muscle activity produced by its prey of shrimp, freshwater crabs and other invertebrates. Echidnas may also be able to detect their prey in this way.

FLOATING RESTAURANT
Platypuses store their prey in cheek pouches, then eat while they float on the surface. Because they do not have teeth, they crush their food between the tongue and horny plates inside the mouth.

Watertight
The platypus keeps its eyes and ears tightly closed while it is underwater.

Webbed feet
Platypuses use only their powerful front feet for swimming.

SMOOTH SWIMMER
The platypus is perfectly adapted for an underwater life. It has webbed feet and fur that holds a layer of air next to the skin for warmth. Its bill detects prey in crevices and on the river bed.

WET AND DRY
On land, the platypus pulls back the webs on its front feet so that it can use its claws to walk and to dig burrows.

A PERPLEXING MIX

When the first specimens of a platypus were sent to England in 1798, many zoologists believed this strange creature was a fake, made of different animals sewn together. They believed it was impossible for one animal to have a duck's bill, an otter's body and a beaver's tail.

STICKY BUSINESS
The short-beaked echidna's tongue is four times as long as its snout and is covered with sticky saliva. It picks up thousands of ants, termites and other small insects during a day's feeding.

Digging claws
Short, strong front limbs equipped with thick claws allow the short-beaked echidna to break into the cement-hard nests of termites.

Fur coat
The echidna's coarse fur stops it from losing heat. Sharp spines, which can be raised or lowered by special muscles, protect it from predators.

Poisonous spur
Male platypuses use the spur on the hind foot in fights with other males.

SINKING FEELING
Echidnas burrow straight down into soft soil to escape attack. They bury themselves until only their prickly spines are visible.

HAPPY WANDERER
Long-beaked echidnas are nocturnal and have large feeding territories. They use backward-facing spikes on the tip of the tongue to "spear" their prey of worms.

Pouched Mammals

ON THE INSIDE
A newly born kangaroo can spend several months in its mother's pouch, where it is warm and protected, before it is able to survive on its own.

There are about 280 species of marsupial. Seventy-five of these are opossums that live in North, Central and South America, while the remaining species, which vary in size, shape and way of life, live in Australia, New Guinea and on nearby islands. They range from mouse-sized honey possums, which eat pollen and nectar, to 6-ft (1.8-m) tall kangaroos, which eat grasses and plants. Marsupials live in many environments, from deserts to rainforests, in burrows, in trees and on the ground. They glide, run, hop and swim, and eat plants, insects, carrion (the flesh of dead animals) and meat. All marsupials have pouches, although some are very small. Because the young are born at an early stage of their development, they shelter in the pouches and feed on their mother's milk until they are old enough to be independent.

PIGGYBACK
Although the koala's pouch faces downwards, the muscles inside hold the baby safe while its mother climbs trees. Later, the young koala rides on its mother's back as she feeds on leaves.

DID YOU KNOW?
The expression "playing possum" comes from the American opossum's unusual habit of pretending to be dead when it is threatened by a predator. This tactic seems to work, because most predators will not attack and eat an animal that is already dead.

FINDING THE POUCH
A wallaby is no larger than a peanut when it is born. It makes its way from the mother's birth canal to her pouch, where it will stay warm and safe for the next five to eleven months.

A BOXING BOUT
Most of the 59 species of wallaby and kangaroo live in family groups. In the mating season, the competition between male kangaroos is fierce. They have kicking and pushing contests and the winners mate with the females.

TIGER WITH A POUCH

The last known wild thylacine, or Tasmanian tiger, was captured in 1933 and died in 1936. Since then, despite many supposed sightings, there has been no proof that the species still exists. The thylacine was more of a marsupial wolf than a tiger. Its teeth, head and front legs were very similar to those of a dog, but unlike most dogs, it could not run fast, and it lived alone or in pairs.

IN AND OUT OF THE POUCH

A young kangaroo pushes its front feet and head into its mother's pouch.

It twists around so its head is on the bottom of the pouch.

Then it turns so that it can see out of the pouch, and is ready to jump out.

HIDE AND SEEK
Moles use their noses to find prey. Their stumpy tails are also covered in sensitive hairs so they can detect a predator behind them in their tunnels.

• INSECT EATERS AND BATS •

A Nose for the Job

There are nearly 4,000 species of mammal, and more than half of these eat insects as part of their diet. One group of mammals, the insectivores, eats mostly insects, although some do feed on meat, such as frogs, lizards and mice. The 365 species of insectivore include small mammals such as shrews, hedgehogs and moles. Insectivores are often solitary, nocturnal mammals. They are fast-moving hunters with a relatively small brain, but a well-developed sense of smell, which they rely on far more than their sense of sight. Most insectivores also have long, narrow snouts to sniff out their prey, and up to 44 sharp teeth. Another group of insect-eating mammals, the xenarthrans (pronounced zen-<u>arth</u>-rans), are also called edentates, which means "toothless." The South American anteaters, however, are the only edentates that have no teeth at all.

A PROBING NOSE
The Pyrenean desman is a mole, but it looks like a shrew. It hunts its prey underwater, and probes beneath rocks for insects with its long, flexible snout.

LITTLE DIGGER
A European mole hunts worms and insects underground. It relies on its sensitive nose to smell and feel its prey.

SPIKY DEFENSE
The nocturnal Algerian hedgehog is protected by its spiny coat. It has a short, pointed snout with sensitive bristles, and eats everything from insects to mushrooms.

HANGING AROUND
The South American giant ground sloth, which grew to 20 ft (6 m) long, became extinct in the last 10,000 years. Its five living relatives live in trees and eat leaves. The largest is the three-toed sloth (above), which grows to 2 ft 2 in (67 cm) long.

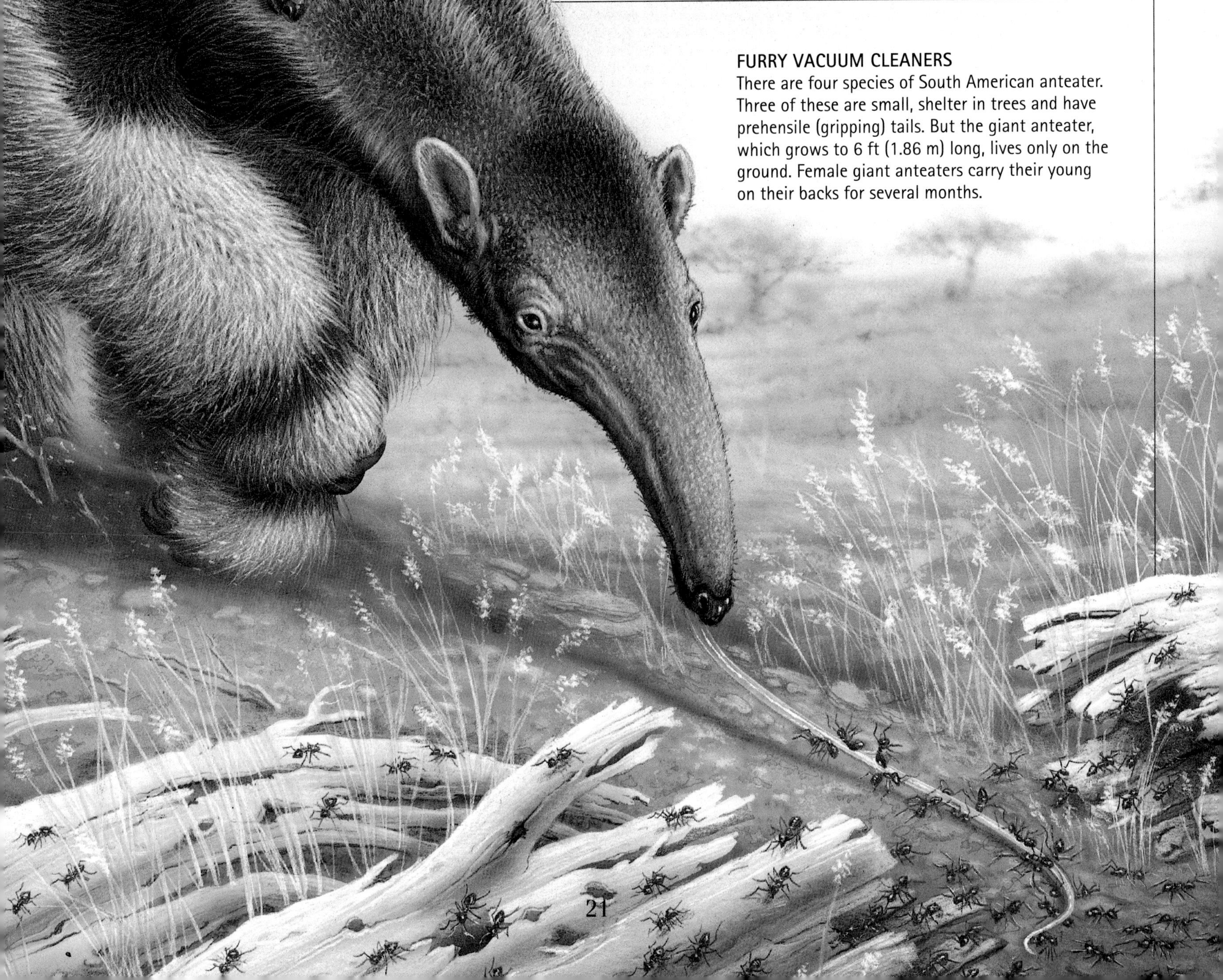

Poisonous Mammals

Two insectivores use venom to help them catch animals that may be larger than they are. The North American short-tailed shrew and the solenodons of Cuba and Haiti produce poisonous saliva to help them subdue struggling prey. They quickly bite their prey and inject it with a small amount of saliva, which causes paralysis. This poisonous saliva is very painful, but not fatal, to humans. Other mammals also use poison. Male platypuses have a poison spur on each ankle, and scientists believe they use these in fights with other males.

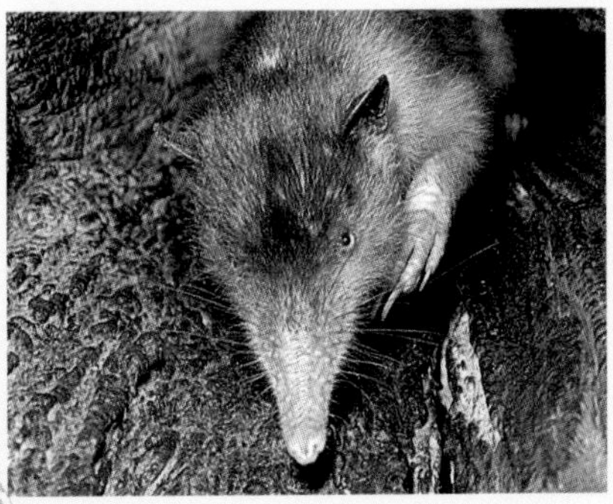

Solenodon

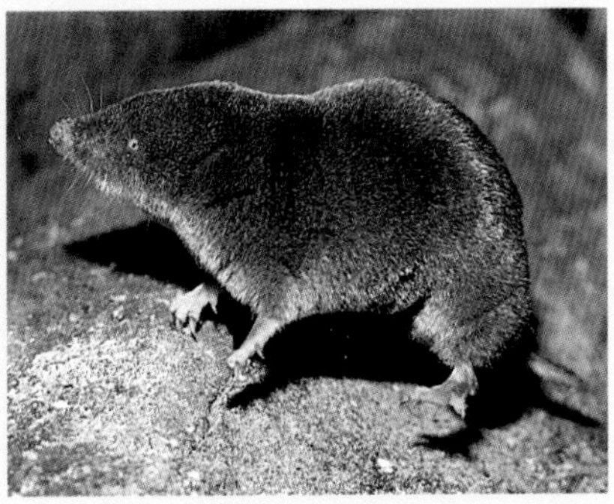

Short-tailed shrew

FURRY VACUUM CLEANERS

There are four species of South American anteater. Three of these are small, shelter in trees and have prehensile (gripping) tails. But the giant anteater, which grows to 6 ft (1.86 m) long, lives only on the ground. Female giant anteaters carry their young on their backs for several months.

Q: Which mole hunts its prey underwater?

VAMPIRE BAT
Found only in North, Central and South America, true blood-drinking vampire bats have razor-sharp front teeth that slice open the skin of a bird or mammal. Their saliva stops blood clotting while they lap up their meal.

BAT FACES
Some bats have long ears and flaps of skin around the nose to detect echoes from prey. Other bats have tube-shaped nostrils that help them sniff out food.

Long-eared bat

Tent-building bat

Lesser bare-backed fruit bat

Hanging Around

About 50 million years ago, a group of insectivores took to the skies, gliding from tree to tree. These gliders evolved into bats—the only mammals that are capable of powered flight. Bats are active mainly at night when there are very few flying predators to threaten or compete with them. They have spread to most parts of the world, except for polar regions and cold mountain areas. Today, there are about 160 species of fruit bat, some of which have wingspans of 5 ft (150 cm), and about 815 species of insect-eating bat, which hunt frogs, fish, birds and small mammals as well as insects. Vampire bats live on the blood of birds and large mammals. Many insect-eating bats eat while they are flying, holding their prey in a special tail pouch. Most bats roost in trees or in caves. Bats that eat fruit and insects use echolocation to navigate and find food. The sounds they make, which are too high for humans to hear, bounce off objects around them.

FLYING FREELY
Free-tailed bats get their name because their tails extend past the flap of skin that joins the hind feet to the tail. There are about 90 species of free-tailed bat, and they are found all over the world. They roost in caves, hollow trees or beneath tree bark.

FRUIT FLYER
Most fruit bats drink the nectar of the fruit and eat its blossoms, but they do not eat the fruit. Some land in trees to eat, but many hover above flowers.

ECHOLOCATION

Most small bats find their way around by using echolocation, which is similar to radar. A bat produces sounds, such as high-pitched squeaks, then listens to the type and position of the echo to detect its prey or its surroundings. It can tell what kind of insect or other prey it is "hearing," and how fast and in what direction that prey is moving. Fishing bats "listen" to ripples on the surface of streams, and can tell which ripples are caused by the current, and which are caused by a fish that is below the surface.

Bat
Produces rapid, high-pitched sounds.

Moth
The bat's sounds bounce off the moth, back to the bat.

PRIMATE HANDS AND FEET
One of the distinctive characteristics of primates is their special thumb (and sometimes their big toe) that enables them to grasp small objects.

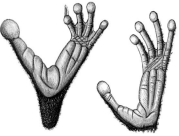

Indri foot	Indri hand

The indri, a kind of lemur, lives most of its life in trees. Its hands and feet are designed to help it climb.

Aye-aye foot	Aye-aye hand

The aye-aye, a kind of lemur, uses its long, thin, second finger to hook insect larvae out of holes in tree branches.

Gorilla foot	Gorilla hand

Gorillas have flattened feet to support their heavy bodies. Their hands are designed to grasp leaves, bark and fruit.

NOSING IN
The proboscis monkey of Southeast Asia has a large nose. It lives on the leaves and fruit of mangroves and other trees.

• PRIMATES •
About Primates

Primates are divided into two groups. The lower primates are lemurs, bushbabies, lorises and tarsiers, while the higher primates are monkeys, apes and humans. Most primates live in trees in tropical regions where their food grows all year round. Many monkeys from Africa and Asia live mainly on the ground in drier environments. They eat a wide variety of food, from seeds and nuts to birds' eggs and nestlings, reptiles and small mammals. Lower primates still have much in common with their insect-eating ancestors. Higher primates, however, have large brains and are quite intelligent. They have good eyesight and binocular vision. They have a highly developed sense of touch because they have sensitive pads on the fingers and toes, and nails instead of claws. Their thumbs are opposable—they can reach around to touch the tips of the other fingers, which helps them to hold and eat food.

EARS AND EYES
Tarsiers live in the rainforests of Southeast Asia. They have large ears and eyes, and leap from branch to branch with their long hind legs as they hunt insects, lizards and small birds. Tarsiers also eat fruit and leaves.

IN THE TREE TOPS

Cotton-top tamarins, which
are found in Central America,
are typical of monkeys from this
part of the world. They live in family
groups and spend most of their lives high in the
rainforest trees, eating fruit, leaves and insects.

INTRUDERS BEWARE!

Primate society is very complex. Some
primates, such as orang-utans, live
alone. Others, such as baboons, howler
monkeys and chimpanzees live in
extended family groups of up to
40 animals. Male gorillas even have
harems of females. Gibbons are highly
evolved apes from South and Southeast
Asia, and the only primates that mate
for life. In this picture, a pair of gibbons
search for fruit, leaves, insects, grubs
and spiders in their own feeding
territory. They "mark" this area every
morning by hooting and howling, which
warns other gibbons to keep away.

25

IN FLIGHT
When threatened, sifakas can run for short distances, holding their arms above their heads. But they return to the trees as soon as they can.

ON PATROL
Waving their tails like flags, a family group of ring-tailed lemurs forages for fruits and insects on the forest floor. Like other lemurs, ring-tails are very social animals and have unusual adaptations for grooming. The second toe on each foot has a claw that they use to clean their ears. They comb each other's fur with the front teeth in their lower jaw.

• PRIMATES •

The Lemurs of Madagascar

Lemurs are unusual, primitive primates. They have ghostlike faces and cry eerily at night. Their name comes from the Latin word for "ghost." Lemurs once lived throughout Africa, Europe and North America, but became extinct in these regions because they had to compete with more advanced monkeys. For the last 50 million years, they have survived only on the African island of Madagascar. There are more than 20 species of lemur. They range from the 11-in (29-cm) long mouse lemur, which includes its long tail, to the 3-ft (90-cm) long indri, with a surprisingly short tail! Most live in the wet forests of eastern Madagascar, where they eat fruit, leaves, insects and small animals such as geckos. Many are nocturnal, and most live in groups of up to 24 animals. All lemurs are endangered because their forest habitat is being destroyed.

CLOSE RELATIONS
Indris are one of the families of lemur. They feed on fruit and leaves, and have to hop on the ground because their hind legs are much longer than their front legs.

DID YOU KNOW?

After a cold night in the Madagascan forests, ring-tailed lemurs stretch out in the trees and sunbathe. When one side of the body is warmed, they turn over and do the other side.

AYE-AYE

The aye-aye is nocturnal, solitary and shy. Famous for its bad smell, it is found only on Madagascar, although a similar species once lived in eastern Africa. The aye-aye eats insects and hunts for larvae beneath the bark of trees. It listens for their movements, then bites away the bark and uses its thin second finger to mash them into a paste. Aye-ayes also use this specialized finger to scoop the soft flesh from fruit.

SAFE RIDE

South American spider monkeys use their prehensile tails as a fifth limb to hang on to slender branches as they travel. A baby spider monkey also uses its tail to keep a firm grip on its mother.

OLD AND NEW

Old World monkeys
Monkeys from Africa and Asia have prominent noses with narrow nostrils that face forward.

New World monkeys
Monkeys from Central and South America have flattened noses with nostrils that face sideways.

• PRIMATES •

Monkeys

About 40 million years ago, new kinds of primates—monkeys and apes—began to take over from the lemurs. Today, there are two groups of monkeys: the Old World monkeys, which live in Africa and Asia; and the New World monkeys, which live only in Central and South America. The 80 or so species of Old World monkey include macaques, langurs, mandrills, baboons, guenons, leaf and colobus monkeys. They have thin, forward-facing nostrils and walk on all fours. Old World monkeys do not have prehensile (gripping) tails and many spend a lot of time on the ground. They eat insects and other animals as well as plants. There are about 65 species of New World monkey, including marmosets, spider monkeys, howlers, capuchins and woolly monkeys. They have widely spaced nostrils that face to the sides, and they spend most of their time in trees. Most New World monkeys are herbivores, or plant eaters. They live in family groups and most have prehensile tails.

MOTHER LOVE

Langurs live in peaceful extended family groups of 15 to 25 animals. Young animals are cared for by their mothers and are protected by other members of the group for up to two years.

MORE SNARL THAN SMILE

Mandrills are the most brightly colored of all monkeys. Males have a red nose, an orange beard, and blue, violet and red buttocks. They bare their large, fanglike canine teeth to express anger or aggression.

28

COLOR CODES

Geladas live in families that are dominated by a male and gather in groups of up to 400 animals. They move through large feeding territories in search of grass, roots, seeds and insects. Although geladas look like baboons, they are not related to them. Geladas use color to communicate. The males have a mane of hair and a bright red patch of naked skin on the chest, which they use to attract females and to warn other males away from their mates.

WINTER WOOLLIES

Most monkeys live in tropical climates, but the Japanese macaque (also called the snow monkey) lives in mountains in Honshu (the main island of Japan), which are covered in snow for more than six months every year.

Discover more in About Primates

The Apes

Apes are the most highly evolved primates. There are four
species: the orang-utan, the gorilla and two species of
chimpanzee. Like humans, apes have flattened fingernails,
no tail and an opposable thumb that can move to touch each of
the other fingers. Orang-utans, which live in Sumatra and Borneo,
are solitary animals. They live in trees and eat fruit, leaves and
occasionally small animals and eggs. Chimpanzees and gorillas are
found only in Africa. They live mainly on the ground and walk on all
fours, supporting their arms on their knuckles. Chimpanzees are very
social animals with many different facial expressions and sounds.
They eat fruit, leaves, birds' eggs, insects and mammals such as
antelopes and monkeys. Although gorillas seem huge and fierce,
they are actually peaceful vegetarians. They build nests in trees
each night, safe from predators and away from the cold ground.

TEACHING TOOLS
Apes learn how to use tools and then pass on
the knowledge to their young. Chimpanzees
use sticks as tools to scoop termites out
of their nests.

PROTECTING THE FAMILY
Gorillas move through the mountain
forests of eastern and central Africa
in family groups. Each family is led
by a large silverback male. He warns
younger males away from his mates
and children by standing upright,
roaring and slapping his chest.

LOOKING AT ORANG-UTANS
Male orang-utans (below) grow to 5 ft 6 in (1.7 m) tall, almost twice as large as females. They have broad, flat faces and large cheek flaps.

SWINGING FROM TREE TO TREE
There are nine species of plant-eating gibbon, which are closely related to the apes. These tree dwellers live in Asia in family groups. Males and females are the same size.

TALKING TO CHIMPS

Scientists have found recently that chimpanzees have almost the same ability to learn as we do. They cannot make human sounds, but they can be taught to communicate with humans using special symbols. This chimp, for example, can ask a human friend to play by touching the symbol that means "chase," then running away. Chimps can also be taught to understand spoken questions. If asked "Can you make the dog bite the snake?," this chimp will put a rubber snake into a toy dog's mouth.

Carnivores

There is one large group of mammals called the Carnivora that has adapted special features for a meat-eating diet. The seven families of carnivore, which are found all over the world, are made up of dogs; bears (including the giant panda); raccoons; weasels, martens, otters, skunks and badgers; civets; hyenas; and cats. These carnivores have two pairs of sharp-edged molars called carnassial teeth and digestive systems that can process food very quickly. But few carnivores eat only meat. Most eat at least some plant material. Bears, for example, eat more plants than meat and their carnassial teeth are rounded so they can grind hard stems and seeds. Although many carnivores are social animals, others are solitary. They drive other members of their species from their hunting territories, except during the mating season.

TREETOP SLUMBERER
The red panda lives in trees where it sleeps most of the day. It eats roots, grasses and eggs as well as fish, insects and mice.

CATLIKE CARNIVORE
The Madagascan fossa looks like a cat, but is actually related to civets. It has a flattened face, and eyes that point forward so it can judge distances when it pounces on its prey.

KILLING BITE
Lionesses hunt together and exhaust their prey before killing it with a fatal bite to the throat. They have powerful jaws and huge canine (stabbing) teeth.

DID YOU KNOW?
Indian and African mongooses eat lizards, insects and venomous snakes! They slowly build up an immunity to snake venom so that, eventually, some can even survive a cobra bite that would kill a human.

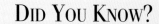

HUNTING FAILURES

Despite their reputations as fierce hunters, most large carnivores fail to catch their prey more times than they succeed. Although cheetahs (right) are the fastest land animals in the world, they are designed for speed, not stamina. If they have not caught their prey within 1,476 ft (450 m), they must give up the chase because they cannot run any further. Lions succeed once in every ten of their hunting attempts, and even large groups of wolves capture their prey only once in every five attempts.

TYPES OF CARNIVORE

Ocelot

Dog

Grizzly bear

Raccoon

Weasel

Civet

Hyena

TABLE MANNERS
Sea otters grow to 4 ft (1.2 m) long, and hunt fish, sea urchins and shellfish. They float on their backs to devour their catch and later, to sleep.

Discover more in Mammal Society

ATTACK AND DEFENSE

Back off
The margay shows it will defend itself by staring with wide eyes.

Ready to attack
The margay gives its enemy a last chance to retreat. It tucks its ears out of the way, opens its mouth wide and shows its sharp teeth.

DID YOU KNOW?
Leopards, which can kill animals as large as a baby giraffe, have very strong neck and back muscles that enable them to drag their prey high into trees to protect it from lions and scavengers.

INVISIBLE HUNTER
A tiger follows its prey silently. Suddenly it leaps, grips the animal with its claws and grabs it by the neck. To make sure a large animal is dead, the tiger bites into its throat so it cannot breathe.

• MEAT EATERS •

The Cat Family

There are 36 members of the cat family. They range from the South American oncilla, which is half as big as a domestic cat, to the Siberian tiger, which grows to 12 ft (3.7 m) long, but they have many features in common. All are hunters, most species eat nothing but meat, most are shy and live alone, and many are nocturnal. Cats hunt in similar ways—stalking their prey silently then attacking in a sudden rush, wrestling their prey to the ground and killing it with a bite to the neck or throat. Most cats use their razor-sharp claws to hold prey, and all except cheetahs pull in their claws so they do not become blunt. Cats have tiny muscles in their tongue so they can change its surface. They groom themselves or their young with a smooth tongue and scrape the skin off their prey with a rough tongue. Sixteen species of cat are endangered, and humans are the biggest threat to their survival.

FISHING CATS

The fishing cat, which grows to 4 ft (1.3 m) long, lives in Southeast Asia and India. It scoops fish out of streams with its webbed paws. It also eats crabs and birds, and has even been known to kill calves, dogs and sheep.

PRIDE OF THE PLAINS

Most cats live alone. But lions are social and live in a family group called a pride, which includes up to 30 animals. Most of these are females (there can be three generations of lionesses in one pride) and their cubs. There are often two dominant males, and they are usually brothers. Young males lead a solitary life until they are older and stronger. Then they challenge the dominant males for control of the pride.

Q: Which is the largest member of the cat family?

• MEAT EATERS •

The Dog Family

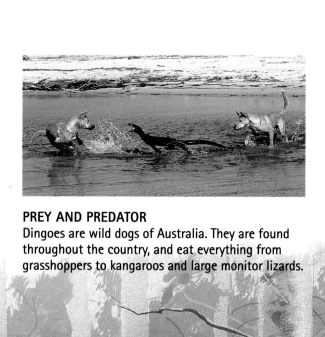

PREY AND PREDATOR
Dingoes are wild dogs of Australia. They are found throughout the country, and eat everything from grasshoppers to kangaroos and large monitor lizards.

Dogs were among the first carnivores, and their way of life, as well as some features of their anatomy, still resembles that of their ancestors of 40 million years ago. They are highly adaptable mammals and are able to take advantage of new habitats and new feeding opportunities. Of the 35 species of wild dog that have now spread to almost every part of the world, 27 species are small, solitary foxes, while the remaining eight species are social dogs that hunt in packs. No matter how they live, all dogs have features in common: keen sight, hearing and smell; strong, sharp canine teeth; and special scissorlike molars (carnassial teeth) that are used for tearing flesh. Dogs are mainly carnivorous, but they also eat insects, fruit, snails and other small prey. Some dogs have evolved to chase prey in open grassland, and one species, the grey fox of North America, even climbs trees in search of food.

DESERT FOX
The cat-sized fennec fox of the Sahara in North Africa has adapted to desert life. It has large ears that help it keep cool by spreading and getting rid of its body heat. Its ears also help the fox to detect its prey moving at night.

DID YOU KNOW?
All dogs protect their young, but African wild dogs care particularly for their pups, such as the one shown here, by providing and sharing food with them.

ON THE PROWL
Wolves are intelligent, efficient hunters that cooperate to tire out their prey. They communicate with body language, facial expressions and howls. The howling chorus of a wolf pack can be heard for about 6 miles (10 km) and tells other wolves to keep away.

As Cunning as a Fox

Foxes have a reputation for being clever because they are quick to learn and to adapt to new habitats. These shy, alert animals are very difficult to approach or trap. They hunt at night and rest during the day in dens, hollow trees or even in drains. Foxes have learned how to survive in cities as well as in the countryside. They eat rabbits, fruit, garbage and pet food.

COYOTE FACES
Coyotes use facial expressions to communicate. They use their ears and mouths to show their feelings, and bare their teeth to express fear and aggression.

Friendly

Submissive

Playful

Attacking

Defending

SUN BEAR
The sun bear of Burma, Sumatra and Borneo is the smallest bear, growing to only 3 ft (1 m). It loves honey, which it licks from beehives with its long tongue.

AN EASY CATCH
Brown bears station themselves at waterfalls on North American rivers and wait for salmon to migrate upstream to lay their eggs. Skilled bears can catch salmon in their mouths.

The Bears

Bears evolved about 40 million years ago in Europe. They spread to Africa, where they are no longer found; Asia; and North and South America. Today there are only eight species of bear. They include the largest of the meat eaters, the polar bear, which can grow to more than 11 ft (nearly 3.5 m) long and weigh 1,600 lb (725 kg), and the slightly heavier North American grizzly. Bears eat anything from plant roots to small and large mammals. Polar bears feed almost entirely on seals and fish, although they can kill reindeer. Bears in colder regions do not hibernate (sleep through winter). When food is scarce, they sleep on and off in dens they dig in hillsides or in snow banks. Females give birth in their dens, where the cubs stay warm until spring. Tropical species, such as the South American spectacled bear, and the Asian sun and sloth bears, are much smaller than their northern relatives.

THE POLAR BEAR'S YEAR

Winter
Females dig dens in snow banks and give birth to their cubs. Males wander along the pack ice at sea and hunt seals.

Spring
The cubs emerge from the den and learn how to hunt. Their mother guards them from predatory males, which will kill and eat the cubs.

Autumn
Bears feed on seals and store fat for winter. Pregnant females move to areas of permanent snow to dig their dens.

Summer
This is the mating season. Polar bears can swim well, and often cross large stretches of open ocean to new hunting grounds.

DID YOU KNOW?

The sloth bear, which lives in India and Sri Lanka, is the largest mammal to feed almost entirely on termites. It forms its large lips into a tube and uses the wide gap between its front teeth to suck termites out of their nests.

GIANT PANDAS

Giant pandas were unknown outside China until the nineteenth century, and are still mysterious animals. Although they sometimes eat birds and small mammals, they live almost entirely on bamboo and spend up to 12 hours a day chewing tough bamboo stalks. As pandas do not digest the bamboo very well, they have to eat up to 44 lb (20 kg) of bamboo a day to survive. Pandas have an extra thumblike structure (part of their wrist bone) on their front paws, which they use to help them grip the bamboo stems.

LIVING IN THE ARCTIC
Polar bears are perfectly adapted to life in the Arctic. They have just enough blood in their feet so their toes do not freeze, and their fur consists of hollow, clear (not white) hairs that trap heat.

Discover more in Carnivores

ELEPHANT'S FOOT
An elephant has five toes on each of its front feet. They are enclosed in a tough, hooflike covering of skin.

ON THEIR TOES
All hoofed mammals walk and run on their toes. Odd-toed hoofed mammals have a middle toe larger than the other toes. Even-toed hoofed mammals walk on their middle two toes.

UNLIKELY RELATIONS
Despite the differences in their appearance and size, hyraxes are the closest living relatives of elephants. Both animals walk on all five toes.

Zebra
Zebras, like horses, run on the central toe of each foot. The other toes are only stumps of bone.

Camel
Camels walk on the third and fourth toes of each foot. The other toes have disappeared.

• GRAZERS AND BROWSERS •

Hoofed Mammals

About 100 million years ago, when plant-eating mammals began to take advantage of open grasslands, they found that the only way they could escape predators was to run. Because it was easier to run on their toes than with a flatter foot, their claws gradually turned into hard hooves, and toes that were not needed for support disappeared or became smaller. Today, there are about 210 species of ungulate, or hoofed mammal, divided into three groups. The primitive ungulates—the elephants, the aardvark, the hyraxes, and the manatees and dugongs (both of which have evolved to live entirely in water)—still have most of their toes. The perissodactyls, or odd-toed ungulates, have three toes (tapirs and rhinos) or one toe (horses and their relatives) on each foot. The artiodactyls, or even-toed ungulates, have two toes (pigs, hippos and camels) or four toes (deer, cattle, sheep, goats, antelopes and giraffes).

DID YOU KNOW?

Camels do not walk on their hooves at all. They actually use their footpads, which give them a good grip on the ground. Their large toes help to prevent them from sinking into the sand.

40

DIGESTIVE SYSTEM

Some hoofed mammals, such as camels, sheep and deer, have complex stomachs (colored green in top diagram) in which they process food. Many can regurgitate the partially processed food from the rumen to the mouth, where they break it down even more with their specialized grinding teeth. This is called "chewing the cud." This food is swallowed again and passes on to the omasum, where nutrients can be absorbed. The animals process food very thoroughly so they can make maximum use of the nutrients it contains. Horses, rhinos and elephants have a simple stomach where they break down their food. They then process it in a very large caecum. They eat large amounts of food, which is often of a poor quality, to get the nutrients they need.

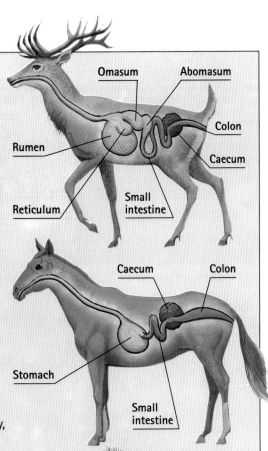

LOUNGING HIPPOS

Hippopotamuses are even-toed ungulates, with four large toes on each foot. Their long, broad toes allow them to walk on the bottom of lakes and swamps as well as on land.

White rhinoceros
White rhinos have three toes on the front foot. The first and fifth toes have disappeared.

Reindeer
Reindeer have four toes, which can spread to provide support on soft snow.

41

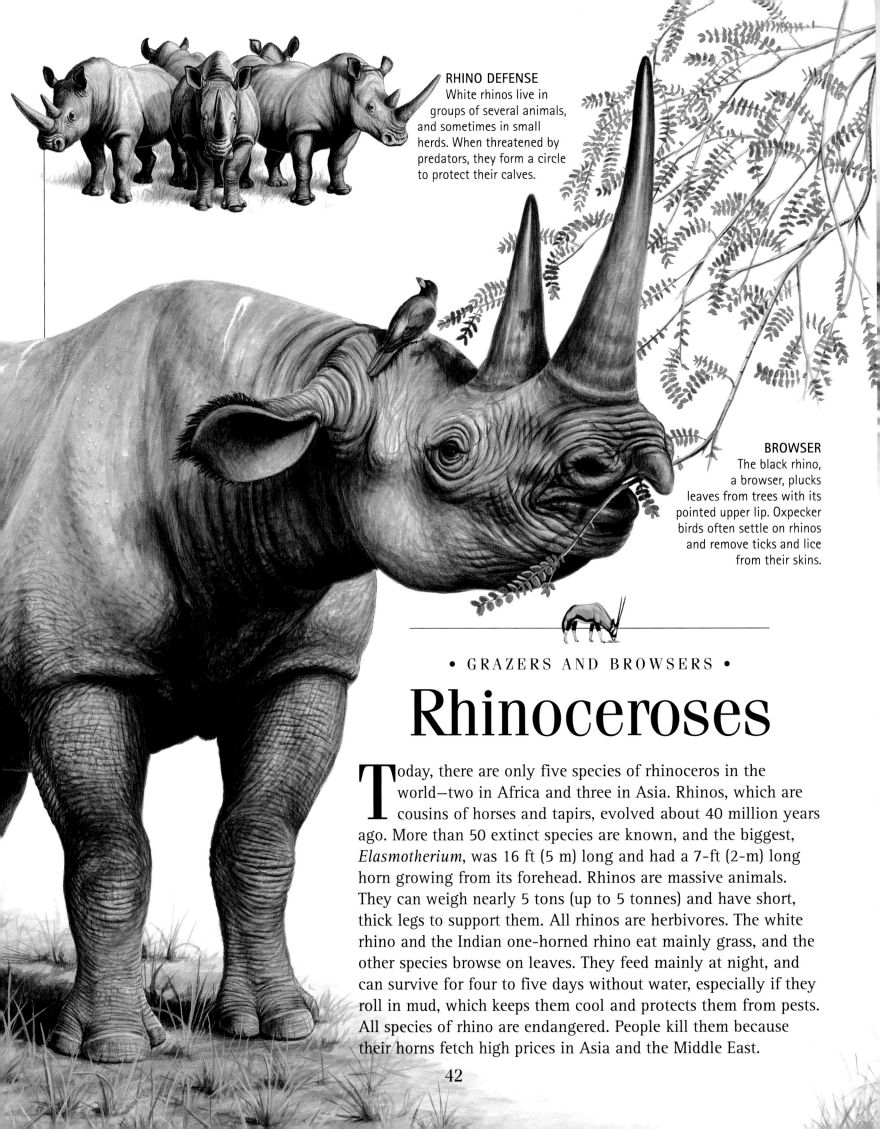

RHINO DEFENSE
White rhinos live in groups of several animals, and sometimes in small herds. When threatened by predators, they form a circle to protect their calves.

BROWSER
The black rhino, a browser, plucks leaves from trees with its pointed upper lip. Oxpecker birds often settle on rhinos and remove ticks and lice from their skins.

• GRAZERS AND BROWSERS •

Rhinoceroses

Today, there are only five species of rhinoceros in the world—two in Africa and three in Asia. Rhinos, which are cousins of horses and tapirs, evolved about 40 million years ago. More than 50 extinct species are known, and the biggest, *Elasmotherium*, was 16 ft (5 m) long and had a 7-ft (2-m) long horn growing from its forehead. Rhinos are massive animals. They can weigh nearly 5 tons (up to 5 tonnes) and have short, thick legs to support them. All rhinos are herbivores. The white rhino and the Indian one-horned rhino eat mainly grass, and the other species browse on leaves. They feed mainly at night, and can survive for four to five days without water, especially if they roll in mud, which keeps them cool and protects them from pests. All species of rhino are endangered. People kill them because their horns fetch high prices in Asia and the Middle East.

Javan rhinoceros
Height: 5 ft 10 in (180 cm)
Horns: males have a single horn up to 11 in (28 cm)
Skin: heavily folded and patterned

Indian rhinoceros
Height: 5 ft 11 in (182 cm)
Horns: single horn up to 2 ft (60 cm) long
Skin: folded, studded with bony nodules

Sumatran rhinoceros
Height: 4 ft 4 in (132 cm)
Horns: two short horns
Skin: folded, covered in red to black bristles

White rhinoceros
Height: 6 ft 5 in (198 cm)
Horns: two horns; front horn up to 5 ft 2 in (157 cm) long
Skin: smooth

Black rhinoceros
Height: 5 ft (152 cm)
Horns: two horns; front horn up to 4 ft 5 in (135 cm) long
Skin: smooth

A RARE RHINOCEROS

The Sumatran rhino, which also lives in Borneo and the Malaya Peninsula, is the most primitive living rhinoceros. It has many features in common with the family's Asian ancestors, such as a hairy body. It also eats bark and lichen as well as leaves and fruits. This species is probably the rarest in the world—only a few hundred survive in the wild.

GRAZER
The white rhino has a broad upper lip that helps it to graze on short grass. Black and white rhinos are actually much the same color—gray. The white rhino is much larger than the black rhino. It is taller, and almost twice as heavy!

Elephants

The first elephants were pig-sized creatures without tusks or trunks that lived in northern Africa about 50 million years ago. Today there are only two species of elephant: the Indian elephant and the African elephant—the largest mammal living on land. Both species live in family groups, which sometimes join to form herds of hundreds of animals. Elephants spend up to 21 hours a day eating as much as 700 lb (320 kg) of leaves, bark, fruit and grass, or traveling in search of food and water. An adult elephant needs to drink 15–20 gallons (70–90 liters) of water a day. Elephants travel through forests on traditional paths called elephants' roads. These intelligent animals have good memories and can live for more than 60 years. Both Indian and African elephants are endangered because humans take over their habitats for farming and poachers kill them for their tusks.

DID YOU KNOW?

An elephant's trunk is strong, sensitive and flexible. It can pull a whole tree out of the ground or pick up a single twig. The trunk does not have any bones, but contains about 150,000 bands of muscle.

HEAT AND DUST
Elephants stay cool by spending several hours each day in water, or by sucking water into their trunks and spraying it over their bodies. They also coat themselves with mud and dust to protect their skins from sunburn and to keep insects away.

BEAST OF BURDEN
Indian elephants are strong and calm. People have used them to carry logs, cattle, food—even soldiers into battle—for thousands of years.

SPOT THE DIFFERENCES

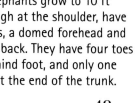

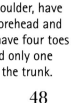

African elephants grow to 13 ft (4 m) high at the shoulder, have large ears and a sloping forehead, and their hips are as high as their shoulders. They have three toes on each hind foot, and two "fingers" at the end of the trunk.

Indian elephants grow to 10 ft (3.2 m) high at the shoulder, have small ears, a domed forehead and a sloping back. They have four toes on each hind foot, and only one "finger" at the end of the trunk.

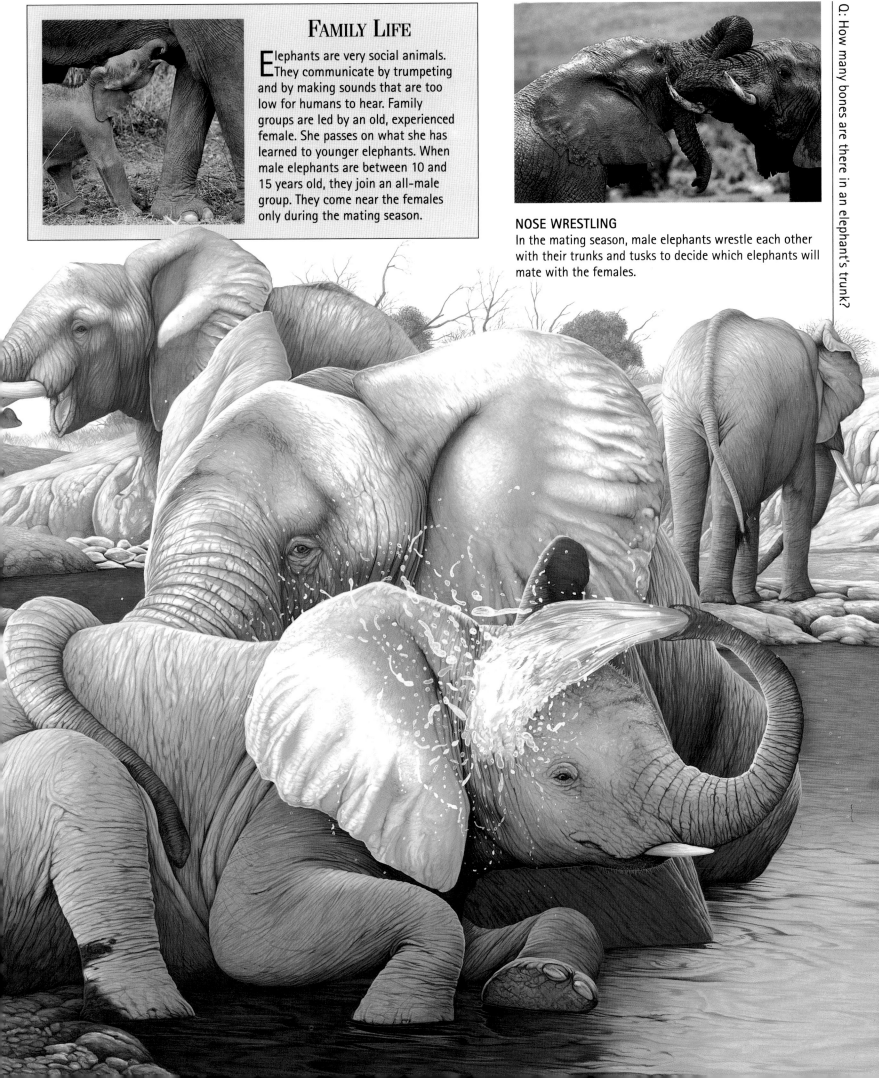

FAMILY LIFE

Elephants are very social animals. They communicate by trumpeting and by making sounds that are too low for humans to hear. Family groups are led by an old, experienced female. She passes on what she has learned to younger elephants. When male elephants are between 10 and 15 years old, they join an all-male group. They come near the females only during the mating season.

NOSE WRESTLING

In the mating season, male elephants wrestle each other with their trunks and tusks to decide which elephants will mate with the females.

Q.: How many bones are there in an elephant's trunk?

Deer and Cattle

GROWING ANTLERS

Early spring
Covered in soft skin called velvet, the antlers bud from beneath the fur of the deer's head.

Late summer
Nourished by blood vessels inside the velvet, the antlers grow to their full extent. New points, or tines, are added every year or so.

Autumn
The velvet dries and is rubbed off against rocks and tree trunks. The deer uses its shiny antlers to let other males know it is ready to fight for control of the herd.

Winter
After the mating season, the antlers become brittle at the base, and are easily knocked off against trees.

Deer and cattle live in most parts of the world, from the Arctic tundra to Southeast Asian rainforests. They range in size from the cat-sized pudu to the North American moose, which can reach more than 7 ft (2 m) at the shoulder. All deer and cattle are herbivores and most eat grasses, leaves and fruit, although caribou eat lichen and moss. There are 38 species of deer, and 128 species of cattle, including sheep, goats, buffalo and the pronghorn antelope. Cattle evolved only about 23 million years ago and have very efficient digestive systems. Many species of cattle have been domesticated. Cattle, sheep and goats have horns that grow throughout their lives. Although the water deer of Asia has tusks, most male deer have antlers that are shed each winter and grow again in spring. They range from simple spikes to racks with many branches. Males fight with their antlers, and the strongest wins control of the herd.

A CLOSED CIRCLE
Musk oxen, which live in the Arctic, are related to goats. When threatened by predators such as wolves, the adults form a protective circle around the calves.

RUNNING FROM DANGER
The Indian nilgai is a medium-sized antelope with short horns. Nilgai rely on speed to escape predators such as leopards and tigers.

SMALLEST OF ALL
The pudu of southern Chile (below) is the world's smallest deer. It weighs 13–15 lb (6–7 kg). The mouse "deer" is smaller, but it is related to antelopes and is not a true deer.

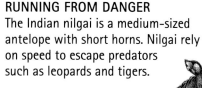

LOCKING IN TO WIN

The antlers of all deer are designed so that they rarely become accidentally entangled. Male caribou lock antlers, then push to see which is stronger. The winner mates with the females of the herd, while the loser waits for another chance to prove its strength.

ODD ONE OUT

Scientists have traditionally put the North American pronghorn into a family of its own because it has many peculiar characteristics. Like cattle, it has horns, not antlers; but like deer, it sheds the outer layer of its horns each year. Today, many scientists include the pronghorn in the family that contains cattle, sheep and goats.

Q: Which is the smallest deer?

DESERT DWELLERS

Gerbils live in the deserts of Africa and Asia. They belong to the mouse family, which is the largest mammal family. These small, nocturnal seed eaters are well adapted to desert life. They get all the water they need from their food and never need to drink.

BEAVERS AT WORK

There are two species of beaver—one in Europe and one in North America. Both species eat bark and leaves and live in water. Beavers protect their large nests, called lodges, by damming streams to form ponds that predators cannot cross.

Rodents

More than a third of all the world's mammals are rodents. From the pygmy jerboa, which could fit into a matchbox, to the capybara, which grows to 4 ft (1.25 m) long and weighs 110 lb (50 kg), rodents live in almost every environment, from the Arctic to the desert. Some species spend almost all their lives in trees, while others live underground. Several species, including beavers, spend much of their time in water. Rodents have many predators. Few species apart from porcupines can defend themselves, and most produce large numbers of young to ensure the survival of their species. Rodents' incisor, or front, teeth grow constantly, ready to gnaw into hard-shelled nuts, tree bark or other plant food. Some rodents eat insects and other small animals as well as plants. Others have special diets—bamboo rats, for example, feed almost exclusively on bamboo.

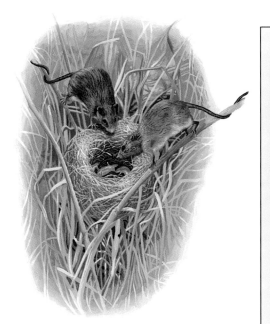

TASTE TREAT
Harvest mice eat grain and seeds and build their nests in long grass or fields of wheat. People in ancient Rome and in China once cooked and ate harvest mice as snacks!

CITIES ON THE PLAIN

Black-tailed prairie dogs, a type of rodent, live on the treeless plains of western North America. They hide from predators and protect each other in "towns." These huge complexes of burrows can cover 75 acres (30 hectares) and house more than 1,000 animals. Each burrow is occupied by a family—a male, three females and about six young. One of the adults stands guard at the mouth of the burrow to warn the others if a predator such as a coyote, fox or hawk approaches.

TYPES OF RODENT
There are many species of rodent, but they look fairly similar. Their behaviour and habits, however, vary greatly.

Capybara

Lemming

Black rat

Crested porcupine

ESCAPE PLAN
A hare's long hind legs give it the speed to avoid predators and the ability to change direction to confuse a hunter such as a hawk, which cannot make sudden twists and turns as quickly.

• BURROWERS AND CHEWERS •

Rabbits and Hares

Rabbits, hares and pikas are called lagomorphs. The 65 or so species of lagomorph live in most environments in Africa, Europe, Asia and the Americas, but they have also been introduced to other parts of the world by humans. They are similar to rodents, but are also different enough for scientists to place them in a separate order. Unlike rodents, lagomorphs have hair on the soles of their feet, but do not have sweat glands. Like rodents, however, lagomorphs' eyes are set at the side of their heads so they can see predators approaching from above and behind, and their gnawing incisor teeth keep growing. Pikas live in deserts and mountain areas in Asia and North America. They have small ears and look a little like large lemmings. Rabbits and hares, however, have long ears, long front legs and very long hind legs, which they use to run and hop. All lagomorphs eat plants, and most emerge from their nests at sunset to feed.

BIG EARS
The black-tailed jack rabbit lives in North American deserts. Its large ears contain hundreds of tiny blood vessels that radiate heat and help the rabbit keep cool during the day. Such big ears also help it hear predators approaching.

54

PIKAS
Pikas are short-legged relatives of rabbits and hares. They collect large amounts of green plant material in summer and dry it in the sun to make hay. They store the hay in their burrows to provide food through the long winter.

FIGHTING FIT
Arctic hares breed in spring. Males and females chase each other and have boxing matches. This gives each hare a chance to see how healthy and strong its potential mate is.

POPULATION EXPLOSION
Lagomorphs are preyed on by many predators. Like rodents, they give birth to many young so that at least some will survive to breed. European rabbits were introduced into Australia in 1788, but they did not begin to spread until 24 wild rabbits were brought to the country in 1859. Within 10 years there were at least 10 million rabbits, and they have plagued Australia ever since.

THE FAMILY BURROW
European rabbits first evolved in northern Africa. They live in burrows called warrens, which protect them from the weather and predators. Female European rabbits give birth to several young up to six times a year. They keep them warm in grass-lined chambers.

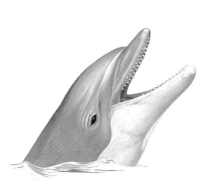

BOTTLENOSE DOLPHIN
This dolphin is a fast swimmer. It has up to 160 small, pointed teeth and feeds on small fish, eels and squid.

MINKE WHALE
The minke whale has 230–360 baleen plates each 8 in (20 cm) long in its upper jaw. It feeds on herring, cod, squid and krill.

SOUTHERN RIGHT WHALE
Named because it was considered "right" for hunting, this whale has 500 baleen plates in its upper jaw. It feeds on krill.

SPERM WHALE
Largest of the toothed whales, the sperm whale has up to 50 teeth in the lower jaw only. It feeds on squid and octopuses.

• MAMMALS OF THE SEA •

Whales and Dolphins

Today's whales and dolphins, which include the biggest mammal that has ever lived—the blue whale—evolved from ungulates (hoofed mammals) about 65 million years ago. Whales, dolphins and porpoises are now perfectly adapted to life in the sea. They have sleek, streamlined bodies and a flattened tail that propels them through the water. Like all mammals, they feed their young on milk. Whales come to the surface to breathe air through a nostril—called a blowhole—on the top of their heads. There are 63 species of toothed whale, which range from the 59-ft (18-m) long sperm whale to 5-ft (1.6-m) long dolphins and porpoises. They feed on squid, fish and octopuses and, like bats, use echolocation to navigate and to find their prey. Some migrate long distances. Baleen whales have no teeth. They use long, hairlike sieves called baleen to strain their food (mainly small fish and shrimp called krill) out of the water. The 11 species of baleen whale roam the world's oceans and migrate when the seasons change.

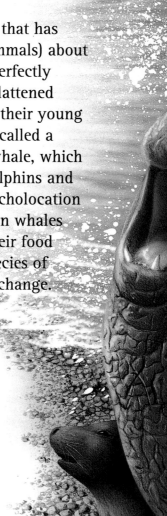

SPEEDY SWIMMERS
There are 31 species of dolphin. Their fishlike shape, smooth skin and flattened tails mean they can swim at high speed without using much energy. Some dolphins have been recorded swimming at 25 miles (40 km) per hour for several hours.

KILLER WHALES

Orcas, or killer whales, are the largest and most intelligent dolphins. Like wolves and lions, they hunt their prey together. An orca, for example, sometimes frightens seals by coming right up onto the beach. The startled seals try to escape into the sea, where other orcas are waiting to catch them.

WHALE TALES

The blue whale grows to 96 ft (29.4 m) long and can weigh 98 tons (100 tonnes). Its mouth is 19 ft (6 m) long, and its heart, which is the size of a small car, pumps 9.5 tons (9.7 tonnes) of blood around its huge body.

Sperm whales have the largest brain of any animal. It is about six times heavier than the average adult human brain. Sperm whales are deep divers and can dive more than 5,000 ft (1,500 m) beneath the ocean's surface.

The narwhal, which lives in Arctic waters, grows to 15 ft (4.5 m) in length. The male has one tusk (and rarely, two) up to 8 ft (2.5 m) long, growing forwards from its snout.

Humpback whales "sing" long, complicated songs that can last for more than an hour and can be heard up to 750 miles (1,200 km) away. Scientists believe humpback whales sing to let other humpbacks know where they are and whether they are males or females.

Humpback whale tail

Q: What is the largest toothed whale?

RIVALS
Male seals, sea lions and walruses become very territorial in the breeding season. They fight each other for the chance to breed with females, which they control in groups called harems.

• MAMMALS OF THE SEA •

Seals and Walruses

About 50 million years ago, mammals that resembled today's sea otters were amphibious: they lived both on land and in the water. Gradually, they began to spend more time in the sea. Their front and hind legs shortened and became flippers. They grew larger and developed a thick layer of fat to protect them from cold oceans. By 10 million years ago, they had evolved into pinnipeds: seals, sea lions and walruses. Today there are 14 species of sea lion, or eared seal, which have small but visible ears, and which can turn their hind flippers around to walk on land. There are also 19 species of "true" or earless seal, which cannot turn their hind flippers, and move like caterpillars on land; and one species of walrus. Pinnipeds are carnivores. They eat crabs, fish and squid. The leopard seal of Antarctic waters also hunts penguins, while walruses, which live in the Arctic, use their tusks to find shellfish and crabs. Pinnipeds breed on land in colonies that can number thousands of animals.

HALF THE SIZE
Male elephant seals, the largest of all seals, reach 20 ft (6.1 m) in length and weigh 3.9 tons (4 tonnes). Female elephant seals (above) are half the size of the males.

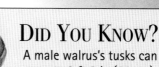

DID YOU KNOW?
A male walrus's tusks can grow to 2 ft 3 in (68 cm) long. Walruses use their tusks to rake shellfish from mud in shallow waters, to pull themselves out of the water onto ice floes, and to battle other males for control of females.

58

SEA LION LIFE
Australian sea lions often hunt squid or fish together. Superbly adapted to life at sea, they can swim a month or so after being born. When they dive, their heartbeat slows from about 100 beats a minute to as low as 10 beats a minute.

DECEPTIVE LOOKS
Manatees (right) and dugongs may look similar to seals, but they are not related. In fact, their closest living relatives are elephants. These sea cows have a smooth, fat body shape and their flippers are similar to those of seals. Unlike seals, however, manatees and dugongs give birth in water, not on land.

BEACH CULTURE
Walruses are social animals that gather in colonies of up to 3,000 in the breeding season. A fully mature male walrus, which can reach 12 ft (3.65 m) in length, may have a harem of as many as 50 females.

Endangered Species

At least 27 species of mammal have become extinct in the last 200 years, and more than 136 species are rare or endangered. Some species, such as snow leopards, tigers and other big cats, have become endangered because their skins are valuable. Others, such as wolves or cougars, have been killed because people think they are dangerous. The Hawaiian monk seal and several species of baleen whale have almost been wiped out for their fur or meat. Most endangered mammals are threatened because their habitats have been destroyed by logging, clearing or draining for farmland.

Northern hairy-nosed wombat

Black-footed ferret (North America)
The black-footed ferret (found from Canada to Texas) is endangered because agricultural practices, such as the poisoning of the prairie dog, have robbed the black-footed ferret of its main prey.

Hawaiian monk seal (Hawaii)
There are two or three species of monk seal. The Caribbean monk seal may already be extinct, and the Mediterranean

Hawaiian monk seal

monk seal is threatened by pollution. The Hawaiian monk seal is endangered because many thousands were slaughtered on their breeding grounds in the Hawaiian islands. The population of Hawaiian monk seal seems to be recovering, but so little is known about this species that we cannot be sure if it will survive.

Northern hairy-nosed wombat (Australia)
Living in dry, open country rather than forests, the northern hairy-nosed wombat was never as widespread as the common wombat. In fact, it was unknown until 1869. It was once found from southern New South Wales to central Queensland, but it disappeared shortly after European settlement. It is now found in eastern Queensland, which is only one small part of its former range.

Giant panda (East Asia)
Giant pandas have always been uncommon because they do not breed very often. The species has become endangered in the twentieth century because they are hunted for their skins and meat, and their habitat is destroyed for farming. Many pandas starve when the bamboo on which they depend flowers and dies every 50 to 100 years.

Wisent (Europe)
Standing 7 ft (2 m) at the shoulder, the wisent, or European bison, is Europe's largest mammal. The species became extinct in the wild when the last

Golden lion tamarin

animals were killed in eastern Europe in the 1920s. Some survived in captivity, however, and animals from captive herds have since been successfully reintroduced into the wild.

Golden lion tamarin (South America)
Five of the 19 species of tamarin monkey, all of which live in tropical Central and South America, are endangered. As some species became popular as pets, thousands were trapped and shipped to other countries—a voyage that killed most of them. The golden lion tamarin, however, is endangered because its forest habitat is being logged and cleared for farmland.

Northern right whale
The northern right whale, the rarest of the baleen whales, was almost extinct in European waters by 1700. By 1785, a North American right whale hunting company had closed down because there were not enough northern right whales left to hunt. Even today there are probably only a few thousand right whales in the world.

Orders of Mammals

Monotremata
Monotremes are reptile-like mammals that live in Australia and New Guinea. There are three species of monotreme: the platypus, the short-beaked echidna and the long-beaked echidna.

Marsupialia
Marsupials, or pouched mammals, live in North and South America, Australia and New Guinea. There are about 280 species, from opossums to koalas and kangaroos.

Xenarthra or Edentata
There are 29 species of anteater, sloth and armadillo. They eat leaves or insects and are found in Central and South America.

Pholidota
The seven species of pangolin (scaly anteater) live in Africa and Southeast Asia. They are all protected by hard, scaly skin.

Insectivora
There are 365 species of insectivore, including tiny shrews, moles and rat-sized hedgehogs. Insectivores live on all continents except Australia and Antarctica.

Macroscelidea
The 15 species of insect-eating elephant shrew, which spend almost all their time on the ground, are found only in Africa.

Scandentia
The 16 species of tree shrew, which live only in Asia, are insect eaters that have features in common with primates as well as insectivores. Only one of the species is nocturnal. The rest feed during the day and night.

Dermoptera
The two species of colugo (flying lemur) both live in Southeast Asia. Their name is misleading because they are not lemurs and they glide, not fly, from tree to tree.

Chiroptera
This is the second largest order of mammals. There are 977 species of bat, with wingspans ranging from 4 in (10 cm) to 5 ft (1.5 m).

Fruit bat

Primates
Most of the 201 species of primate are monkeys, tarsiers and tree-dwelling prosimians, such as lemurs. The apes are the largest of the primates.

Carnivora
Meat-eating or carnivorous mammals are found on almost every continent. There are 269 species, including 34 species of seal, sea lion and walrus.

Tubulidentata
This order has only one species: the short-legged, long-nosed aardvark. This pig-sized anteater is found only in Africa, south of the Sahara Desert.

Sirenia
The four species of manatee and dugong are found in the warm, shallow waters of the western Pacific and Indian oceans; in North, Central and South America; and in the rivers of West Africa.

Hyracoidea
There are eight species of rabbit-like hyrax. They live in Africa and the Middle East and share some features with elephants.

Proboscidea
There are only two species of the largest living land mammals—the elephant. One lives in Africa, the other is in Asia.

Perissodactyla
The 16 species of horse, tapir and rhino—the odd-toed ungulates—are native to Africa, Asia and South America.

Artiodactyla
There are 194 species of even-toed ungulate, including pigs, deer, camels, hippos, antelopes, giraffes, sheep, goats and cattle. They are native to every continent except Australia and Antarctica.

Cetacea
The 77 species of whale, dolphin and porpoise are found in all the world's seas. There are also five freshwater species of dolphin.

Lagomorpha
There are 65 species of rabbit and hare. They are native to Africa, Europe, Asia and North and South America. They were introduced into Australia and the Pacific islands.

Rodentia
This is the largest order of mammals, with 1,793 species. They are found all over the world except Antarctica.

Note: We have divided mammals into 20 orders. Some scientists believe there are only 16 orders of mammals, while others say there are as many as 23 orders. This is because taxonomy, which is the study of classifying animals, changes as scientists learn more about mammals and how they are related to each other.

African buffalo

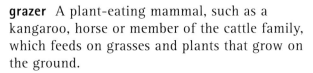

Glossary

Sun bear

Uakari

Joey in kangaroo pouch

Fur seal with harem

Langur monkeys

adaptation A change that occurs in an animal's behavior or body to allow it to survive and reproduce in new conditions.

artiodactyl An ungulate, or hoofed mammal, that has an even number of toes. An artiodactyl has either two toes, such as camels; or four toes, such as deer, cattle, sheep, goats and giraffes.

browser A plant-eating mammal that uses its hands or lips to pick leaves from trees and bushes (for example, koalas and giraffes) or low-growing plants (for example, the black rhino).

carnassial teeth Special teeth with sharp, scissorlike edges used by carnivores to tear up their food before they swallow it.

carnivore An animal that eats mainly meat. Most carnivorous mammals are predators, or hunters, while some are both hunters and scavengers. Most carnivores eat some plant material as well as meat.

convergent evolution The situation where different, unrelated kinds of animals in different parts of the world evolve to look similar because they live in similar ways.

Cretaceous Period The period from 145 to 65 million years ago. It was during this period that marsupials, monotremes and placentals first appeared.

echolocation A system of navigation used by some animals that relies on sound rather than sight or touch. Dolphins, porpoises and many bats use echolocation to tell them where they are, where their prey is, and if anything is in their way.

edentate A placental mammal, such as an armadillo, anteater or sloth, which belongs to the order of mammals called the Edentata.

endangered In danger of becoming extinct. A plant or animal can become endangered because of environmental changes or human activities.

evolution The gradual change, over many generations, in plant or animal species as they adapt to new conditions or new environments.

extinct No longer surviving. At least 27 species of mammal have disappeared, or become extinct, in the last 200 years.

grazer A plant-eating mammal, such as a kangaroo, horse or member of the cattle family, which feeds on grasses and plants that grow on the ground.

habitat The home of a plant or animal. Many different kinds of mammal live in the same environment (for example, a rainforest), but they each live in different habitats within that environment. Some mammals in a rainforest live in the trees, while others may live on the ground.

herbivore A mammal that eats only plants. Some herbivorous mammals eat leaves, bark or roots. Many of the ungulates eat only leaves.

hibernation A long period of very deep sleep. Some mammals eat as much as they can before the winter, then curl up and sleep in a sheltered spot. They live off the fat they have stored, and they slow their breathing and heartbeat to help conserve their energy until spring.

insectivore A mammal that eats only or mainly insects or invertebrates. Some insectivorous mammals eat meat, such as frogs, lizards and mice.

invertebrate An animal that does not have a backbone. Many invertebrates are soft-bodied animals, such as worms, leeches or octopuses, but many have a hard external skeleton, such as crabs and beetles.

Jurassic Period The period from 208 to 145 million years ago. During this period, the mammals remained quite small. They did not change much from their ancestors of the Triassic Period. All of these mammals are now extinct.

lagomorph A rabbit or hare. Although lagomorphs are similar to rodents, they also have important differences. A lagomorph, for example, has hair on the soles of its feet and does not have sweat glands.

mammal A vertebrate that is warm-blooded, suckles its young with milk and has a single bone in the lower jaw. Although most mammals have hair and give birth to live young, some, such as whales and dolphins, do not have hair, and others, the monotremes, lay eggs.

marsupial A mammal that gives birth to young that are not fully developed. These young must be protected in pouches (where they feed on milk) before they can move around independently.

monotreme A primitive mammal with many features in common with reptiles. Monotremes lay eggs. There are only three species of monotreme, the platypus and two species of echidna, all of which live in Australia and New Guinea.

multituberculate An extinct group of mammals that lived in the Northern Hemisphere. They looked like rodents, but were not related to any of today's mammals. They became extinct about 50 million years ago.

nocturnal Nocturnal mammals are active at night and sleep during the day. They have special adaptations, such as large, sensitive eyes and ears, or long whiskers, to help them find their way in the dark.

omnivore A mammal that eats both plant and animal food. Bears and many primates, including humans, are omnivores. They have teeth and digestive systems designed to process almost any kind of food.

opposable thumb A thumb that can reach around and touch all of the other fingers on the same hand.

perissodactyl An ungulate, or hoofed mammal, that has an odd, or uneven, number of toes. A perissodactyl has either three toes, such as tapirs and rhinos, or one toe, such as horses and their relatives.

pinnipeds Mammals such as seals, sea lions or walruses, which have evolved fan-shaped hind flippers instead of feet. They use these to propel them quickly through water with very little effort.

placental A mammal that does not lay eggs (as monotremes do), or give birth to young that must be cared for in a pouch (as marsupials do), but which nourishes the developing young inside its body with a special organ called a placenta.

predator A mammal that only or mainly eats other animals. Predators are mainly carnivorous, or meat-eating, animals.

prehensile Grasping or gripping. Some tree-dwelling mammals have prehensile feet or tails that can be used as an extra limb to help them stay safely in a tree while feeding, climbing or sleeping. Elephants have a prehensile "finger"

on the end of their trunks so they can pick up small pieces of food. Browsers, such as giraffes, have prehensile lips to help them grip leaves.

Koalas

prosimian A primitive primate, such as a lemur, bushbaby, loris and tarsier.

regurgitate To bring food back up from the stomach to the mouth. Many hoofed mammals use this process to break down their food into a more liquid form. This is called "chewing the cud."

scavenger A mammal that eats carrion (dead animals)—often the remains of animals killed by predators.

Pangolin

social Living in groups. Social mammals can live in breeding pairs (a male and a female), sometimes together with their young, or in herds of thousands of animals.

solitary Living alone. Solitary mammals usually meet other animals of the same species during the breeding season. At other times they avoid each other's company.

White rhinos

synapsid An animal that has a single opening in the skull behind the eye socket, which is used to anchor strong jaw muscles. Mammals are descended from synapsid reptiles.

Triassic Period The period from 245 to 208 million years ago. The first mammals appeared towards the end of this period.

ungulate A hoofed mammal. There are three groups of ungulates: elephants and hyraxes; the perissodactyls, or odd-toed ungulates (horses, zebras, hippos and tapirs); and the artiodactyls, or even-toed ungulates (camels, cattle, deer, sheep and goats).

vertebrate Having a backbone. All vertebrate animals have an internal skeleton of cartilage or bone.

Harvest mice

warm-blooded An animal that can keep its internal body temperature more or less the same, regardless of the outside temperature. Both birds and mammals are warm-blooded.

xenarthran Another scientific name for a member of the order Edentata.

Humpback whale

Index

Picture Credits

(t=top, b=bottom, l=left, r=right, c=center, F=front, C=cover, B=back, Bg=background)
Ardea, 32c (B. Arthus), 36tr (J.P. Ferrero), 21c (P. Morris).
Kathie Atkinson, 17br. Auscape, 45br (E. & P. Bauer), 15tl (T. De Roy), 17bc, 25br (J.P. Ferrero), 15tc, 46bc, 46bl, 61br (Ferrero/Labat), 60tl (A. Henley), 7tr (Jacana), 61tc (Jacana/Photo Researchers/M.D. Tuttle), 16tcr, 18bc, 19tr (D. Parer & E. Parer-Cook). Australian Museum, 10tr. Australian Picture Library, 55tl, 26tl, 43tr (Minden Pictures), 12bc (Minden Pictures/F. Nicklin), 18tl, 54tcl, 54tl (ZEFA). Bruce Coleman Limited, 29tr, 50c (F. Bruemmer), 20tl (J. Burton), 48cl (G. Cubitt), 30tr (P. Davey), 20br (F.J. Erize), 53tc (Jeff Foot Productions), 49tl (D. & M. Plage), 7tcr, 59tcr (H. Reinhard), 51tr (J. Shaw), 15tr, 35tl (R. Williams), 26br, 27bl (K. Wothe), 12tl (G. Zielser). The Image Bank, 38tcl (P. McCormick), 7tl (J. van Os). Images of Nature, 38/39c (T. Mangelsen). International Photographic Library, 33tc. Magnum, 31br (M. Nichols). Mitchell Library, State Library of New South Wales, 17tl.

NHPA, 9cr (H. Ausloos), 49tr (A. Bannister), 41tr, 44tl (N.J. Dennis), 28bc (K. Schafer), 32tr (M. Wendler), 31tc (A. Williams). The Photo Library, Sydney, 13tr (N. Fobes/TSI), 37tc (K. Schafer/TSI), 29br, 46cr, 55tc, (A. Wolfe/TSI). Planet Earth Pictures, 13br (R. Coomber), 36cl (A. Dragesco), 47cl (K. Lucas), 40tcl (K. Scholey), 56bl (J.D. Watt). Tom Stack & Associates, 21tr, 59tr (D. Holden Bailey), 7cr (B. Parker), 8tl (R. Planck), 60bl (E. Robinson), 60tr (D. Tackett), 35tr, 39tr (B. von Hoffmann), 58bl (D. Watts). Merlin D. Tuttle/Bat Conservation International, 22bc, 22tl.

Illustration Credits

Alistair Barnard, 24cl. André Boos, 3, 4bl, 32/33c, 32bc, 32l, 33r. Martin Camm, 1, 28tc, 28cl, 28bl, 34tl, 34cl, 48/49c, 48bl, 56t, 57tr, 62bl, 62tcl. Simone End, 6bl, 6tr, 18cl, 19br, 38bl, 38tl, 39tl, 54/55c, 54br, 55tl, 58/59c, 58bc, 58tl, 62bcl, 62cl, 62tl, 63tr. Christer Eriksson, 6/7c, 18/19c, 28/29c, 34/35c, 56/57c. Tim Hayward/Bernard Thornton

Artists, UK, 2l, 12/13c, 12bl, 13cr, 63br. David Kirshner, 8/9b, 8cl, 9tc, 9c, 9tr, 42l, 42t, 47t, 47r, 63cr, 63tcr. Frank Knight, 4/5c, 36/37c, 36bl, 37r, 40/41c, 40tc, 40tl, 41tc, 41cr. John Mac/Folio, 20/21c, 20tc, 20bl, 22/23c, 22cl, 22bl, 23tr, 50/51c, 50l, 50b. James McKinnon, 24/25c, 24tc, 24bl, 52/53c, 52tl, 53tl, 53tr, 63bcr. Trevor Ruth, 14/15b, 14tl, 43–46c, 46br. Peter Schouten, 4tl, 5br, 5tr, 10/11c, 10tl, 10bl, 10bc, 11tr, 11tcr, 26/27c, 30/31c, 31tr, icons. Kevin Stead, 16c, 16bl, 16tr, 17tr. Rod Westblade, endpapers.

Cover Credits

Auscape, Bg (M. Freeman). Simone End, BCbr. Christer Eriksson, FCc. John Mac/Folio, FCtr. The Photo Library, Sydney, FCcr (A. Wolfe/TSI). Kevin Stead, BCtl.